Palpitations

By:
Jonathan

Palpitations
Book Nine of the Series *The Nine*
May 22, 2018, *First Edition*

Copyright © 2018

Cover Photo Credit: Saffu

All rights reserved. This book or any portion thereof may not be reproduced or used in any manner whatsoever without the express written permission of the publisher except for the use of brief quotations in a book review or scholarly journal.

ISBN-13: 978-1-942967-37-8

KreativeMinds Publishing
www.kreativeminds.net

Ordering Information:

Special discounts are available on quantity purchases by corporations, associations, educators, and others. For details, contact the publisher at the above listed address or the email address below.

U.S. trade bookstores and wholesalers: Please use the email address below. email: publishing@kreativeminds.net

To Lord God Almighty, through whom all things are possible.

Always,
Jonathan

Introduction

...

The words encased within this book are a collage of thoughts, sustenance, and substance intended not just to be read, but rather to be studied, ingested, and allowed to find resonance within the soul. Whether through poem, song, or succinct thought, this book is intended to seek a place of rest and actualization within those who seek truth. Some people may identify with poetry, others through melody, while others may identify through succinct thoughts – for art is the method of communication through which words embrace another's soul. In whatever way a person identifies with truth, the delivery of the message housed within the words of this book should be seen in a way similar to how each star in the great ocean of stars serves as a gentle twinkling of truth and direction – beacons calling the soul home.

Always,
Jonathan

...

Invocation

Father,

King. Almighty Lord. Take all that I humbly am and use it for Your will – Your great intentions. Through these words, allow Your Spirit to saturate the pages. Allow the thoughts of the reader to dance gracefully around in song with the words, becoming lost in an eternal waltz with You. Through these words, may the great truths that I have humbly been allowed to bare witness to find uncolored resonance within those that seek You. May their souls become engulfed in the dauntless wonder and beauty that shall one day unfold before them. May they find Love. May they find You. You are my All, my Heart, my Eternal. In Your Most Holy Name – forever and in all ways.

Amen.

PART 1

Palpitations

Of Palpitations

These palpitations of my heart resonate deep within the foundations of my soul. The words are a movement within the mind – a way to conceptualize thought; to invoke art unto words that have been granted life to reside within. May these palpitations find counterpoint within the souls of others and humbly awaken those able to hear to the great calling of the Divine Creator of All. Blessed be Thee for through Thee I am blessed and through Thee I am enabled to allow my hand and pen to serve as a vessel in the delivery of these words. The beautiful chamber of the Eternal echoes throughout the ethereal fabric of my humbled existence and through these words I dedicate these palpitations unto Thee.

...

Part 1 | Palpitations

Awake

Awake – I am
In a way I did not choose
Open to the visceral intentions that are predicated
Upon reason and understanding of which I cannot comprehend.
Fathoms dividing the chasm between inspiration and
Dissonant derivatives of wandering hope
What will stand to prevail?
Unto it has yet to be seen
Aye, for my inner struggle has turned external
My faith is wielding a sword to battle
But a dark knight has come to slaughter.

Blind

I close my eyes
Mind enveloped in a state of andante
A glint of beauty hiding
Behind the shearing of opaque white
The notes from a piano gently ringing,
Ping-pinging to a transcended reality

Palpitations

I am truly blind
And only in these moments –
Is our reality recognized as a façade,
In just but a flick in our linear timeline
I am forever.

I Heard You Laugh

I heard you laugh
I heard happiness
I heard the better part of life resonate in that moment
Dancing around in my head
And more importantly, my consciousness
I could have experienced that moment
One thousand times over and it would never get old
Or one thousand years and I would still yearn to hear it again
I was enraptured in its effervescence
My very being electrified
Every facet of my soul charged
Captured by only a laugh
But invigorated through the unintended ripples
That rocked me through the depths of my core.

Part 1 | Palpitations

Jacob's Ladder

Sublime is the kingdom that has gone undiscovered
By the doers of the literal Words mistaken.
The darkest of hearts entangling its roots in the language
Both writ and spoken, falling short of intentions.
A distortion of truth − yet a truth unmeasured
For its secrets still lie in the stability in all of our presence.
Through a mantle of white and the most exotic of lights,
Only this will lead you to the ascent of Jacob's ladder.

Snowflakes

Glass
Delicate and divine
To the observer, a matrimony of chill and dew on high
Gently falling.
And to the Creator, the source of life's beautiful dance with phi.
An ode of majestic perfection
Wisping down from the temporal stitching of the sky.

Palpitations

Surfing the Sky

Surfing the sky, catching the break on a cloud
Riding the cusp of the water our atmosphere has bound.
A glimmer a glint – all wondrous in hue
I am light.

Timeless Waltz

There she was.
Subtle in the way she first grabbed my attention.
Charging the very air of each breath I would take –
A timeless waltz with the fabric of my essence.
It was in that moment I was entangled in a predetermined certainty
So vastly ineffable from every fairytale with which I was raised.
All I had known was lost in an overwhelming sense of purpose.
Though even with no aforementioned guidance or direction
I somehow knew I was right where I needed to be
Enveloped and enraptured, and never a word even spoken.

Part 1 | Palpitations

Tin Man

A tin man stands at attention
Almighty in stance, triumphant in mystique.
A sordid ambiguity to a sense of meaning
Hiding behind a rusty shield of broken emotions
That time is only beginning to wither at the seams.
Grain by grain of the hour glass falls
Woe the tin man has been all but hollow,
For hollow is all he's allowed to be seen.
A false visage to absorb the weather –
One day,
Some day
He will really be seen.
I am tin man.

Dancing Lights of Azure

I close my eyes to dancing lights of azure
Striations in a familiar landscape closing in
It's hard to breathe – suffocating in between
But here I am –
There she is, welcoming me again.

Palpitations

Beautiful-amazing.
She takes my breath away.
And then I realize I no longer need to breathe here
Awestruck, in a word, permeates my soul
The very essence of Love.
Love – she is Love; a visual manifestation of Love's majestic radiance
Alas I am tethered to a world of time and another without
My compass has led me here
A reminder of home
And she is.

A Walk of Remembrance

A walk of remembrance,
A destiny awaiting its day.
It is not too simple to believe that we are part of a greater plan –
A plan somehow in that everything we do,
Right or wrong and all along
Is right where we are supposed to be.
Nothing spoken
Nothing broken
Only the mercy of how we acclimated to it all
The ebb and flow to the winding road of Grace.
Ground breaking beneath our feet –
A journey notably changing amidst our motion's wake.

Part 1 | Palpitations

Solace

A solace within and a blue lake outside
Those days of the sounds dancing around
The inner mind, the heartbreak
And finding Love again
There are angels – guardians of our lives
Persistently shaping – and without judgment –
A day when ego will cede priority to notice
Of the astounding visage of the very IS around us
And therein granting us serenity in hope;
To dance the shores of the blue waters;
To see the unseen.
Tranquility, Love and peace.

Everything

Fading
Waiting
Quietly feigning to a great awakening
Only once will it all rise to a grand denouement
And within that once is a moment of everything –
Grand design simplified

Palpitations

One point
One moment
Everything.

Reminisce

Seeing her silent pleasantry in the same vein
As the graceful manner in which she entered
Noticed not I how fleeting the moment would be
She laughed
She said it had been a while for me
Puzzling over the line, I came to realize
It was I who entered and not the other way around
A secret journey designed to fool even me
A secret destination with a fervor so familiar
For it is where we'd believe we would be
The omnipresent, and all along where we will return
I said hello
She smiled
Her loving eyes locked in the deep gaze of mine
It was then when we again began to reminisce.

Part 1 | Palpitations

Picasso's Stars

Stasis
The place between two extremes
The plumb line between the pendulum swings
An ode to Serenity from Eternity's calling
A symbiotic balance culled with a spiritual awling
Forever in a moment through the lensing of the bees
A fleeting journey to Picasso's stars
All woe! The brevity of a dream.

A Butterfly's Nod

A butterfly landed on my arm
Soot-black with a bluish hue
A tender look of recognition – it knew I knew
As if on queue, music playing in the background cut right through
The words, His words, spoke to me:
"Whoever you turn out to be
You're forever part of me
You turn me to a father from a son
All we are, you are
And who we'll be, you'll be

Palpitations

Love and hurt, doubt and trust
Welcome to being one of us"
With a hint of acknowledgement
A nod of his head
A glimmer in the moment, so subtle, so grand
And with that, the butterfly took flight to the wind.

A Beautiful Message*

Beautiful beings
In the forms of the stars
So simple, so elegant
Still learning who you are
We're not so distant
Though you see us from afar
We're among you, the eternal
To remind you, "You are."

*spoken through me on 7/13/13 around 11:13am CST

Part 1 | Palpitations

Primordial Sonata

Flight
Take off and ascension
No different than any dreamer's intention
Leaving the earth, a typical inclination
But for what purpose, what motivation?
It is so for our light inside calls for departure!
The boarding gate disguised as a mortal martyr
Yet alas the dreamer is atypical in nature
A recognition within of a desired separation
A journey to the stars
Or a guardian encounter?
A yearning to hear the primordial sonata.

Blue Marble

A Western lily overture and lilac symphony
Performing to the score of its own cacophony
A horn section muted in humbled Azaleas
A limelight of beautiful adoration
African starlits sparkle with wonder
And all of this from our little blue marble

Palpitations

To be keenly aware of the bigger intention
Is the mark of clarity and candid separation
A kingdom, a land, a locale of disposition
The human mind is capable of such a vision
The grandeur of the unseen alluring at rest
The simplest path to ethereal Everest

Child

Child-eyed and reiteratively
I couldn't help but continue to ask of Thee
For help in understanding the precursors to before
Those times that led us to this rapport
For faithfully budding in the spirit's bloom
Leaves many un-answers on the whim of the moon
But who am I to question?
Or perhaps a greater question remains…
Who am I, and was I, when I let go of the reigns?

Part 1 | Palpitations

Couture

Antiquity
Serendipity solemn
Erring on the side of solitude befallen
Penchants of innocence in a rustic desolate
A hidden discipline in allure
Beauty not withstanding
Yet magnificence effervescing
A secret veiling amidst a soul's couture

Afterlife's Prose

An island
The surroundings picturesque of the unknown
On blue wonder does it all but exist alone
The island's awareness incomplete on its own merits
An unconscious embodiment cast from conscious limits
Greatness and grandeur oiling perception of stature
A brazen propensity void of the hereafter
Oh to be seen from the view of Oblivion's edge
Washed in the awning of the light of Is.

Symphony

What if the world as we know it isn't as it seems?
What if reality exists only in our dreams?
What if the people we know and the interactions we seek
Are with the other lost souls finding their peace?
What if our life in this world is not our first round ever?
What if the true world existed both before and after?
What if the truth of the matter is the inverse that is preached?
What if we're intentionally lost until we're ready to see?
What if the echoes of direction that "we are so it shall be"
Are the heirs from a murmur of ego's deceit?
All we are is because it was and will forever be
Bound to the angelic concord and eternal symphony.

Leilel's Invocation

Ruby fire razen on the horizon
Daylight fading away
To be the last to feel the final rays from the sun touch my mortal skin
As the Earth roles away its attention to another day
Away to the land of eternal dreams

Part 1 | Palpitations

On Leilel's invocation and beseech
A gentle reminder of the bearings of this incantation
And the soul's zealous will to surmise the invitation
A journey to the stars, beyond human vernacular
To a mesmerizing melding of astral spectacular
Blending of colors – a palette veneer
Invoking a primal call of navigation
To be home
To be here

Guardian

Silence.
A gentle rumble and I am here –
Eyes open.
Brilliance, light;
A visceral spectacle debonair
Eyes level with the great crossed arms of the guardian eternal
His gaze stern and unwavering
Yet an acknowledgement I am there
He will fade or he will stay
His decision…
My fate.
A stay and I enter
A fade and I wake.

Blue Achtung

Blue, baby blue
Starlight-wondrous hues
Irises, no words mistaken
Could have possibly spoken unto
Brilliance in artful candor
Iridescence in shades of Vishnu
A truth poetic
In Her eyes
Blue Achtung

Alien Owl

Alien Owl
Wisdom eternal
Orbis eyes glowing with a lion's bellow
Oh wise vessel, your presence reveres
A call to the conscious-Akashic
Past knowledge ordained in zeal
Your eyes unveil a wondrous truth

Part 1 | Palpitations

A window into a dimension beyond
Facets of a dream-state reality
A celestial carriage – from the aether, drawn

Perspective

A barge drifting down the rainbow highway
Society's impetus to drift along
Aimless in wanton ambition
Feigning intuition's root
Containment and confinement, constricting their bubble reality
The basis of a blind eye turned, ergo affinity's obsolescence
Cavernous perspectives lure the occupants' perceptions
As a distraction to the dreamer's ponder
But for those who choose to stand alone,
Strong in curious vision
The chance of a question asked, an answer given
Will render a window of perspective.

Warrior

Blonde
Streaks of Magnificent painting the contours of her visage
An unmistakable angelic homage
Halo crystal eyes of such glassy-blue
The allure: the cusp of an aurora's azure hue
Deeply drawn in –
An enchanted land
Gravity gratifying so grand
A release of the ballasts, I'm crashing in.
She knows not the power her eyes hold
She wields a Love confounding
The toughest warrior's requite untold.

Of Noetic

Light.
Sound.
Color.
It is all interconnected –

Part 1 | Palpitations

Bridging the mind unto Divinity's rampart covenant.
A world within the bounds of our own
Flickering into focus
All for a moment
Countering the intent of brevity's purpose
A parallel jaunt to a sojourn existence
Flittering, splintering into
Fractals of noetic sentiment

Bound

She said stop
I paused.
Frozen, holding my breath
My heart beat a thousand times over
She placed a finger on my lips as if to hold my words in
She said nothing; I no longer had words
She stood there, bare – her soul naked before me
Inches between us
A world forming around us
All of my life I had never felt Love like this
All of my Love had never felt life like this
We were running as fast as we could toward each other
Separated only by time, unbeknownst to each other
And here we were – found.

Palpitations

Bound.
In the way she looked at me
Eclipsed in the way I looked at her.

The Horizon

How you save me over and over and over
Falling pieces of me
Tumbling
Tangled
Melting
Meteorite igniting
Heeding to a star-crossed rescue
Saving, reeling
On the cusp of....

Be

Stay.
Stand beside me and be my strength
Stand behind me and be my will

Part 1 | Palpitations

Stand in front of me and be my confidence
Stand within me and be my heart
For the four winds in time will blow
And fuel the soul to move
Unto thee I am blessed to be
Deliverer of Thou's desire
Vessel of divine servitude
Born from humbled beginnings
So that Ye may never cease to be

Ascended

Up into the light
My eyes have seen
The spirit of Divine presence
So clear, so keen
My eyes are open
My mortal body remains
An homage of the Lord's eternal Love-divine
Ascended unto the nectar of His Prestige

Palpitations

Allure

Svelte
Silhouette accented
A visceral imagery of her own volition
She had not a form
That was human in nature
Spellbound; awestruck in eternal aether
She was young, old, strong, meek
She was everything I have ever and never seen
Her eyes were kind, wise, a fire alive
They spoke words like a finely aged wine
Her beauty called to a white horse rising
Ascending into a light ever-blinding
All allure
All intrigue
Forever drawn into her mystique
She was everything
Is everything
The very song played within
A dance on the strings of my heart
An angelic symphony of hymn

Oils

Ardent adventures
Of such verdant valor
The Valley of Kings
An opus apostle
Pouring within
The oils of the Eternal
Cleansing the soul
Of the weary traveler's honor
Washing the feet of man
A symbolic washing of the soul within
The oils an accent unto
Divinity's ardent land

Chic

The remembrance of classy
Grace, elegance of last
And blundered beginnings
To humbled happenchance
Parting ways through pardon
Plundering the gates within

Palpitations

Through chic forgiveness
Of a soul's will to live and experience
But define not ye through the ways of the external
The exterior shall shine
When the soul goes to battle
Not through the graces of candor
Will evidence remain
A shabby, chic splendor
Of the soul entrains

Salted

Oh spice divine of the ever eternal
For you are the preserve
The eternal candle
The wick that is found within each of us
Bound deep inside the soul's earthly mantle
Shan't it be we are but a vessel
To the flicker inside — a reminder of the anvil?
A pertinent truth so precious against our vanilla
An angelic riptide salted with Your Presence

Part 1 | Palpitations

Midnight-Red

She was midnight-red
Smoky exterior, sultry physique
All emotions enchanting
Instilling herself on the hearts and minds
To anyone choosing to see
But lest not her mystique lure the mind
Away from the important seed found hidden inside
A humbling reminder of exterior's trials
A call to the Order
To let her know you know
The real reason she stands before you is not as it appears
Her cloak and veil drift down to her feet
Standing bathed in a triumphant white-revere
A noble light blinding
Her true spirit revealed

Echoes

Something to hope for –
Something to believe in
A found stillness within, every time restlessness descends

Palpitations

And in that moment when life seems so out of tilt
Find reason to Love
And let down the walls that guard from the Love of another
Lest the echoes of the past continue to haunt the mind
Inhibiting the very Essence, the Internal, the Eternal
Divine.

Fell Into Mine

She spoke not in words, but in spirit
And though the words may have echoed from her lips
I was enchanted by a conversation silent
A silence so profound that my soul responded helplessly in kind
In ache – with a tremble, a tremor, a wake;
I have to believe it registered at the outermost edges of the heavens
An epicenter that all began when her eyes fell into mine.

Strong & Statin

I was caught up in the moment
Enraptured in what could be
Maybe she'd say, "Yes"

Part 1 | Palpitations

And we were standing on the edge of destiny
Woe perhaps it would be another ill-fated ending
But whatever the case may be, one truth spoke clear
Words, strong and statin
In her answer, His truth revealed

Omniscient Destiny

Every time I allow my heart a chance
A gasp of air from the depths of suffocation
My lungs are filled with hope
Longing
A lingering question of desire
Blind to knowing His plan
A trust unspoken
That in His will is what will be
A great awakening within
One foot in front of the other
Perhaps it will not be my time to run
Or perhaps the race has already begun
A series of missteps and blunders
Or fortunes-to-be
A brief uncertainty
But in faith I shall surrender reason
For in faith is our omniscient destiny

Palpitations

Beaches of Morrow

Sinking into the sand
Slowly submersing into the depths of something solid
Yet clearly able to move freely about
With the motion the wind may choose
A promise of a grand tomorrow
An end and a beginning of burning blue
On the edge of divinity's furnace
Radiating from the beaches to the horizon
Overflowing in the crystalline glow of the aether
That shines forth from the scattered shards of perfection
Laying across the Beaches of Morrow

Essence of Her Amazing

At the thought of amazing
My mind races spectacularly
At speeds blinding, binding
Chasing the limits of time and space
A simple thought multiplied by the thousands

Part 1 | Palpitations

A thousand hopes
A thousand dreams
A thousand times a thousand
Seams that bind the cover to the pages of a classic novel
With every reading, descriptions of
A piece of her anew
Her very heart
Her very Love
The very essence of her amazing

Quintessence

Everyday is a fairytale
When there is nothing to hide
And God is your only guide
Leading you through
His strength bleeding within you
When every interaction
Every chance for something new
Follows a script He's penned for you
A storybook of yore untold
Enchanting miracles to unfold
The effervescence of His presence
The ever-after of the fairytale's quintessence

Harbinger

Thought.
Racing through the galaxy at a speed greater than light
An instant in knowing
An all-seeing eye into the cosmos
The divide between two locales
The seen and the unseen
Everything illogical is optical
The thought tantamount to Divinity's sheen
A sheet, a veil
Wafting through the chasm –
The great divide between two peoples
Each awaiting a harbinger of hope
A being to journey between the two extremes

PART 2

Melodies of the Heart

Of Melodies

A melody of the heart is more than an emotion, more than a feeling, more than a combination of words strung together into a thought. A melody of the heart is a thought that moves throughout the body, evoking feelings from the surface all of the way through to the core – imaginative words of rhyme, candor, and artful phrasing that move as a melody dancing with the soul. These are the melodies of my heart – some broken, some of Love, some of thoughtful desire, some of allure.

The melody of the heart has no boundaries and is only seen for what it is when the recognition of the moment is captured by the pen. The words hold fast to no hard truth – only motion of the thought and in the way it moves. And in almost all of the written context, the Love expressed is not of this Earth – but in the feeling of seeing and interacting with the angels that come in the night, and who are with us unseen throughout the day. Sometimes She is seen through another's actions. Sometimes She is seen through another's life. Sometimes, She just Is. And in that, all I will ever know is how humbled I feel to experience a Love so grand.

Palpitations

To see, to feel, to understand just a small portion of what a perfect Love feels like, leaves the Earthly experience empty at first – that is until one can begin to see the manifestations of the great Love permeating throughout all that surrounds and has been created within the world…but most importantly, to see Her in another. For it is only then, the experience of interacting with the angels transcends into the experience of everything that Is, veiled from the eyes of those not yet ready to see. So these are the melodies of my heart, a book of Love, a book of Hope, a book of the night, a book unto the Light.

...

Part 2 | Melodies of the Heart

Broken Halo

I see a halo around her head that no one does
The world can think she won't amount to very much
And perhaps think she is the kind of person to lead another on
But there's so much more to her that eyes cannot see
She's just a broken halo trying to find her way home
She's doing all she can just to get by on her own
She's a little jaded and oh so underrated
If you can take the time to see
She has a broken halo and she deserves the very best from me

Hallelu

You are Amazing Grace
Wonderful tonight
Rock-a-bye like a Lullaby
For it was always you
It was only you
In all ways and for always
Hallelu, Hallelu-jah

Capsized

She's the rain on a tin roof in a passing storm
She the wind whistling through the dark
She's the smell of honeysuckle on a springtime morn
She's autumn leaves falling whimsically in the park
And now I'm surrendering
I'm fading
Veins racing
I'm dazing in and out of reality
This insanity
It has wrapped me up in
I've capsized within

Not So Cinderella

It's not so Cinderella
At least not in the way we've been told
It's not happily ever after
In the way we've come to know
It's so much more than we could have ever been known.
So I won't blink.
I'm walking toward the Door

Part 2 | Melodies of the Heart

Something so beautiful
A wanderlust I've never felt before
Lord I think I'm losing my mind
It's not so Cinderella this time

Twilight

His first real goodbye
Her first real cry
First time first Love comes to an end
But she will get on with her life
Slowly passing by on the chance
That Love could come back again
Yeah, no one is ever really ready for it to begin
It wasn't that he was wrong
And it wasn't that she was right
Only the hope of the open road that comes
To a fork in the dead of night
Though Love remains
Such a Love of the grandest kind
No words, but forever held in her eyes –
The remnants and streaks of a lost Love's Twilight

Home

This is my Love song to You
Oh how You've made me come unglued
You are the tide racing through my veins
Every time I call Your name
Like a ship tossed around at the mercy of a great sea
I've been waiting for You to rescue me
You are the lighthouse guiding me home
I want to be home.

White Flag

She looked over my way
I thought I saw her smile
It was enough to linger for a while
This isn't right
This trembling in me
How could she do this just by looking at me?
I'm a one man army giving in
My white flag is flying overhead
I've held out for just about as long as I can
So now, I'm crashing in

Part 2 | Melodies of the Heart

Blanket of Certainty

Unbelievable
Indescribable
She's all consuming to me
She isn't just beautiful
And at times, I know I can be a handful
But she's got every piece of me
When I see her I can go on and on
I can finally breathe
She's so amazing to me
She's the beginning of all that was and will ever be
Encompassing me
In an equidistant blanket of certainty

Enrapture

Midnight I lie awake just to watch you sleep
Moonlight falls across your face
I can barely breathe in and breathe out
From the avalanche that has overcome me
It is amazing with you lying next to me
Wrapped up in that white sheet
And nothing underneath

Palpitations

And the scent of your pillow
Reminding me of how you still mesmerize me
You enrapture me

Atmosphere

Something must have told me
In that moment when I first saw you
Something took a hold of me
There was nothing I could do
I can't believe how you captured me
It's amazing
You carry me away
You take me higher
Breathing desire in your atmosphere
Your gravity is holding me in an orbit
Spinning around and around you
You carry me away
On a white wind blazing a whiter day
You carry me away
A mystery is unfolding in a perfect way
Something uncontrollable
Attempting to tempt fate
I've surrendered
Unto shall we enter
Into the walls beyond the Gate

Part 2 | Melodies of the Heart

You Dared Me To Move

I can still hear that goodbye as I watched you fade away
The echoes of those words drift in and out
Pieces of my yesterday scattered among the stars around me
Every piece cuts so bittersweet
So I'll keep moving on
Because you dared me to move
So close to the edge of reality
And now its all encompassing me
Leaving me unwrapped
Unraveling at the seams
In moments of peace and sheer certainty
It's not just ordinary
No book or rules explaining what to do
Just a hint of you peeking through
And oh the beautiful hue
Illuminating the path ahead
The azure journey streaking an uncharted path
Of a destination eternal
Accenting hope to the enchanted unsaid
All because you dared me to move

Palpitations

Isn't She Something

Isn't she quite wonderful
The way she can walk through that door
And take the breath of every guy
She doesn't even have to try
Maybe its the way she moves her hips
Maybe its her smile and kiss-me lips
Maybe its those words I've left unsaid
The thought keeps running through my head
Because isn't she something
She's that woman that gets the best of me
And moves everything inside of me
She's the one that I want for always
And the one I want in all ways
She's a kind words can't describe
Yeah, isn't she something
When that smile falls across her face
There's a chorus of Amazing Grace
My heart rocks from her wake
There was no warning or sign to say
That those come-and-get-me eyes
Would burn right through to my soul inside
That's how I know I'm alive

Part 2 | Melodies of the Heart

I can't get her out of my mind
There's something about her
She's more than amazing
There's a mystery unraveling
How she drives me crazy

All I Need

It's been a long, long ride
There were times I didn't think that we'd survive
But we made it through
Just me and You
And I know, I know that You had your doubts
So many times, You could have just walked out
But You made a stand
You became my helping hand
And Love saw us through
Faith kept us together
No matter what we do
All I need is You
I know, I know that I've hurt You in the past
But I swore that time would be the last
You forgave me
You helped me see
That Love would see us through

Palpitations

And faith would keep us together
No matter what we do
All I need is You
All I need is You

Angels Cry

It feels like I slip farther from You every single day
It is getting harder to call Your name
When I bow my head and pray
I'm scraping through the wreckage
I've harbored all of my lies
No one to tell them to, I'm on the edge of this life
One more step and no one will have to know
Just how hard I've fought not to let go
As they watch me fall the angels cry
They've seen the bloodstains and battles in my life
I'm on a leap of fate racing through the sky
Falling like the tears that angels cry
The chill of the wind cuts through my skin
Free falling from the edge
Its a calm awakening
No bracing for the end
There's no one there to catch me
There's no chance to begin again

I need forgiveness now
God knows how I've sinned
A moment of peace to let me know
That it is okay that I had to let go

Fading Into You

Whatever happened to Love songs
The kind that make you stop right in your tracks
And take someone you know
And for a moment just stop and dance
They're not really played on the radio
And everyone has forgotten the big romance
It's kinda sad these days
Because no songs say it like this:
"I'm caught in your gravity
Spinning around
My core is unraveling
From the inside down
It's quite the sight from this point of view
Because baby, I'm fading into you"
Maybe it's the way the times have changed
Or maybe it's a sign of a song that should be played
To me, or so it seems
To help make a lasting kind of memory

Palpitations

Like the feeling of breath on a neck
The feeling of bodies pressing chest to chest
Where words aren't even said
Because the words to the song say it best
And so it seems from this point of view
I'm fading into you
And I know it's too late
I've lost my grounding
And I'm okay with it
It's quite the sight from this point of view
Because I'm fading into you

Feel My Life Again

Day by day, I'm going through the motions
I've been tossed around in an endless ocean
The tides are raging as I hold on for dear life
To this day I haven't moved on with my life
And even now in these headstrong winds
We could find a way to fight our way through
I'm trying to be strong
Lord I'm crying out to you
To help me carry on
Because everything she was
Made me totally helpless

Part 2 | Melodies of the Heart

And the way she moved me
Would do more than she ever knew
If I could only see her now
I'd feel my life again
Sometimes I can't help but wonder
About the way things were back then

Blindly Beautiful

They say seeing is believing, but I haven't seen a thing
That would lead me another way to believe
I keep getting lost in her, with each chapter
With each tremor, it keeps getting sweeter,
I keep getting weaker for her
It sure doesn't seem like this could be reality
She has the best of me
So let this be and help me see
That a perfect day won't end in rain
A perfect storm won't roll through like a midnight train
I'm caught in the eye of her hurricane
It's all blindly beautiful in her sustain

I'm Yours Always

Someday I should turn around
And leave this guilt and all I've drowned
And find a new way to live
I chased those reckless dreams
Wasted on selfish things
And I lost track of all importance
I've struggled to this day
And I believe I'm moving on
I'm trying so hard to be strong
It's a promise I won't break
There's way too much at stake
Because there will be times You test me
But that's when I'll stand up and say
I'm Yours always
I'm Yours always
Seems like I've been down
For so long I've lost those rounds
Now I have a new match to give
This change was overdue
I'm Yours always

Part 2 | Melodies of the Heart

Insanely Beautiful

I see angels in your eyes
When you smile back at me
I'm still trying to realize
What you really see in me
Because it is plain to see that I
Should be so much more
For you to want to hold on to
Because you're insanely beautiful
To me there is no doubt
You make time find standstill
Just by being yourself
It's a rush words can't explain
Yeah, I'm going insane
Because you're insanely beautiful to me
You unlock the mystery of my life
When you stare back into me
My veins are a rushing tide
I have no uncertainty
You've got me reeling inside
Feeling shaky through and through
To me its just what you do

Palpitations

Kiss-Me Kryptonite

You looked wonderful tonight
The way the moon danced in your eyes
Under the blanket of a starry sky
And I couldn't help but stop and stare
It was the first time I had ever realized
It was the first time in my life
I had been so mesmerized
But that is all it took, I knew right there
Just you and I in the spotlight of the moon shining down
Such a rush in the moment
It felt like no one was around.
It was like the 4th of July
How I was set off inside
Fireworks flashing I was crashing into you
For a moment the world was spinning
Around us at the speed of light
I was so paralyzed
Hypnotized in your kiss-me kryptonite
With every breath I would take
I felt a tremble in the earth's moon
A rushing tide from your wake
And I knew, I was falling for you

Part 2 | Melodies of the Heart

And all along I watched you trying not to hesitate
Barely making the most of a feeling I still can't shake
And I never even blinked
I never had to think
Yeah I never even blinked
Hypnotized in your kiss-me kryptonite
You were too beautiful tonight

How Much She Loved Him

On a wild autumn night
Underneath a stormy sky
All of their hope disappeared
When the doctor's news filled the room with tears
He couldn't fight anymore
And she knew when she walked through that door
She'd have to say goodbye to the one she Loved
She stayed with him till that sun came up
A final tear fell in her coffee cup
She kissed his cheek and was walked away
It broke her heart that she couldn't stay
Then she thought of his words
"I'll wait for you" was the last thing she heard
As the morning's dawn fell across his face

Palpitations

He swore he'd never let go
She knew that he'd always know
Just how much, how much she Loved him
It was hard to move on
Every time she heard their song
And he thought of her all of the time
And often wondered if he crossed her mind
The rain poured down while she prayed
She wondered when time would call her name
She longed for so long to be with the one she Loved
He asked his Father one day
When He'd be passing by her way
Wanted to know when she could come home to stay
He swore he'd never let go
She knew that he'd always know
Just how much, how much she Loved him
He swore he'd never let go
She knew that he'd always know
Just how much, how much she Loved him

More Than Everything

She's all I've ever wanted
She inspires each breath
She leaves my world in balance

Part 2 | Melodies of the Heart

She's every sin I confess
She can be a little stubborn
But for her I'll be my best
Absence wasn't real until she came and filled it
That space in-between my soul and reality
She is more than everything
She's crazy-amazing to me
I can't understand what this rush is
Tilting me upside down and all around
She's my drug and I can't come down
And it seems like there's something I've missed
Because I can't accept
That she's real to me
She is more than everything

Peace of Mind

I know I'll be okay
When I can break these chains
That keep holding me down
And I know the sun will one day shine
When I find some peace of mind
So I'll keep looking for a way
Every single day
To leave the thoughts I create

Palpitations

And the decisions I make
In the earthly wake I will leave behind
Because I know the sun will one day shine
When I find some peace of mind

That's Her

When you find a man that calls you lady,
Beautiful, and baby
And if you're angry and walk out on him
He'll come back to you again
He'll stay awake to watch you sleep
Breathe in every breath you take
And when you don't know how you'll make it
When you wake up, and don't want to get out of bed with him
When you find a man that Loves to kiss you on the forehead instead
And wants to show you off to the world
When you're not even dressed your best
He'll hold hands in front of his friends
Dance with you on a whim
He'll remind you just how lucky he is
When you wake up, without makeup
And you're just as pretty to him
He might spin you around
He might take you again

Part 2 | Melodies of the Heart

He might make you miss the wanting
And say, "Catch me I'm falling"
He's the one who will say in front of his friends
"That's her
I knew it from the moment
I laid eyes on her.
A rush at first blush
Something so fast and so rare
All it took was that first look
I was hypnotized that day
I fell at such a fast rate
I didn't blink
I knew it was all going to be okay
Because, that's her"

The Best Kind of Beautiful

The strawberry sunset matched her margarita
As I watched that summer sun dance across her skin
I couldn't help but feel a little jealous
So much beauty wrapped up in her it felt like sin
She doesn't know that she's so beautiful
She doesn't know what every guy sees
She doesn't know that she's so beautiful
And that's the best kind of beautiful to me

Palpitations

A windy day can do her hair no wrong
Wrapped across her face, those blue eyes peeking through
I get lost in her each time that it happens
Wasting away in that moment as she doesn't have a clue
Because she doesn't know that she's so beautiful

Unraveling

She can tame all the wild I've known
Be a bullet straight to my soul
A passing wave that rocks the boat
Every memory to unfold
She's erasing restlessness
A rambling enchantedness
Yeah, I wasn't looking for this
That's why it leaves me scared to death
Because I think she's more than awakening me inside again
But its alright, I'll be fine
Don't worry about me
I'll catch my breath again
I'll breath in and breath out
And just smile so she won't see
That inside I'm unraveling
When she smiles it's like the sunrise
The kind that leaves you mesmerized

Part 2 | Melodies of the Heart

Its a rush you can't deny
The kind that leaves you more alive
I think she's more than awakening me inside again

Wonderland

It was every best day I could remember
Her eyes and smile could light up the room
That afternoon movie might not have seemed so special
But its not what makes the date, but who
She didn't have to try for me, she already had me
And I'm high, so high
Afloat at the top of this shaky feeling
Melting into pieces
That gravity can't unwind
She's more than amazing
I'm fading
Into her wonderland

Palpitations

You Consume Me

There's something in the air
Something about the way
You walk into the room
The softness of your eyes make me realize
How much you move me
Your breath on my skin makes me come unglued
Without you, I don't know what I'd do
So I'm wondering if you know exactly what you do to me
I'm thinking you could be my everything
Your smile spins me around
Its like I'm high and I just can't come down
You linger on the brink of reality
You consume me
The midday walks, the late night talks
I wouldn't want to go a single day without them
You're a classic movie, the perfect scene
Right past the point of uncertainty
And when you draw near you take my breath away
It's time I let you know – it's time I say
How much you move me
How you consume me

Part 2 | Melodies of the Heart

Song of My Savior

When you say, nothing's the matter
And I say, "You can't be a liar
Because you know I realize
The things you try to hide.
You see just how I know you
When I take you in My arms
And I know you try through the tears you cry
To tell me how you're scared.
Because you see the courage inside of My eyes
Watching and waiting
For you to let all of your feelings inside
Surrender and trust Me."
Then you describe that certain moment
Of when your fears faded away
And I say "I can't promise you more
Than you already see in Me."
And you say these words to Me:
"Do You see the courage inside of my eyes
Embracing the trust of
You setting me off wildly inside
I've surrendered to You completely."

PART 3

Inspirations

Of Inspirations

Through You I am merely but a vessel for these Words, but through You, I Am. The inspirations offered unto those willing to hear, willing to see, willing to understand how blindness and deafness are the unnatural states humans accept as sublime truth, are but a series of guideposts for the soul. The words and phrases – these inspirations – herein hold a directive, a motion of truth to see through the blindness and hear through the deafness that encumbers the human experience. It is but through these succinct thoughts that direction is to be gained and the delta from unknown paths shall begin to take form. May thee who accept these words be blessed with direction and guidance on the path to You upon the Word of the Heavens. With praises lifted up, glory be unto You, the Father.

...

Part 3 | Inspirations

1.

Notice the motion inside of you – the motion that pushes and tugs at your core. That is "being" and is what this trip around the sun is all about.

2.

If you have been blessed enough to be able to give, bless those in need as well – not just those closest to you.

3.

Sometimes the real lesson comes after you think you've learned the lesson.

Palpitations

4.

There are angels around us everyday. Some appear in a way visible only to the eyes of the intended; others through the people encountered... however unaware they may be as a carrier of the spirit.

5.

There is nothing created – only that which has been observed.

6.

Proximity is one of the most misunderstood aspects of life. Stop and take notice of the ripples you create without ever doing a thing.

Part 3 | Inspirations

7.

When the train is a little late to arrive, be patient and know that it's arrival is really right on time.

8.

The world is patiently waiting for you to recognize it has been speaking to you all along; unwavering in wonder for your open eyes and ears.

9.

Blessed be the children – and those who reach out to influence them, for every man, woman, and child are but children on this divine playground.

Palpitations

10.

The hero smiles and the villain doesn't. Be the hero.

11.

To Love like fire; to speak with laughter; to dream within each others thoughts; to look into each others eyes and tremble inside. These are the signs of gravity calling.

12.

Always know that you wouldn't have become today who you were intended to be, if what you thought should've been, actually happened then.

Part 3 | Inspirations

13.

Be still and know that her proximity is near. By time or by distance, the only thing that truly separates us is time.

14.

When a person listens for the unspoken they hear the Creator talking. When they open their eyes to the invisible, everything falls into view

.

15.

Fear is the driver of man's emotions. Faith is knowing what was there all along.

Palpitations

16.

Science and logic got me here. Faith keeps me going.

17.

Every day is a start of something beautiful.

18.

The root of every problem is founded on the divide of one core principle: Love – the division being Love for others versus Love of self.

Part 3 | Inspirations

19.

Everyone wants to succeed, but definitions of success are often misguided. Think not of what you want, but who you can become at the core.

20.

Don't mistake the marvels and gifts of life – the tools you've been provided to help you grow along the way – as your identity.

21.

You only have one identity. Stripped down, naked, and alone on a deserted island, your true identity won't change.

Palpitations

22.

You can't share your life with someone if you can't share your life with someone.

23.

Half moon, blue sky and sun shining down – a perfect day on this third rock.

24.

The art of talking is in listening.

Part 3 | Inspirations

25.

To see people not as humans, but as souls changes the perspective of everything – every interaction, every relationship, every emotion.

26.

All greatness begins in darkness, sometimes without even a pinhole of light to offer hope. It is within these moments that a person is defined.

27.

Too often people judge, obliviously pronouncing their own nearsightedness to the magnificence of everything around them.

Palpitations

28.

Duality. Triunes. These terms compose the core tenets of life and existence.

29.

Within space, distance, and silence the greatest growth occurs.

30.

The quest to understand purpose is often muddied through the lens of careers, oft due to misidentifying identity with career.

Part 3 | Inspirations

31.

The world around you is breathtaking just as is. Sometimes just stopping to soak it in will change the direction of your day.

32.

Engage in the life around you – not getting lost in the hope of what was or will one day be. The moment of now is engulfed in the spotlight.

33.

To give is to do so without expectation of recognition or return. Anything else is bi-directional in effort and fuel for the ego.

Palpitations

34.

Don't bring to public attention what can be taken care of through private intervention.

35.

You can never be taken advantage of if you make decisions willfully – with no expectation of how the decision will benefit or affect your being.

36.

Ever wonder what the inner-voice could have sounded like before the advent of language? Listen for that, for words are only an outward expression of all that is within.

Part 3 | Inspirations

37.

A child believes they disappear when they close their eyes. Who should argue differently? Certainly not the person with eyes wide open.

38.

Though history will probably fail to recognize it as such, the "Material Age" will be seen as a greater advancement than the age of technology, though one could not exist without the other.

39.

Every piece of good and bad is critical on the journey – each group experience, a time of learning. But the most profound growth begins alone.

Palpitations

40.

Anytime the word "I" is spoken in a sentence, stop, pause and realize "you are not." Only in this can a person begin to divest himself from ego.

41.

The space between two notes is where all of the magic happens; the resonance from what was and the anticipation of what could be. Life. Love.

42.

We all need each other, more than most will ever know. In all we seek from our Creator, He answers through the voices and actions of others.

Part 3 | Inspirations

43.

Tucking away the pain doesn't mean it will be ridden from your being. It just means it has been shoveled deeper within and it will take more effort to dig out when the time comes to address it.

44.

Kindness doesn't see a reason – it sees a need.

45.

If you are depressed, you are focused on the past; if anxious, you are focused on the future; if at peace, you are focused on the present.

Palpitations

46.

Breathe in; place one foot in front of the other, for we are all blessed to be part of this journey. Today is breathtaking if you let it.

47.

Don't be afraid to strive for amazing.

48.

Subconsciously, people understand spiritual auras; some people see them with their eyes; but most often, its just a pull or push, to or away from someone.

Part 3 | Inspirations

49.

The higher you rise, the farther the potential to fall. But one must decide to stand up before there is an opportunity to fall down.

50.

I have to believe I am running as fast as I can toward her – whoever she may be – and she's running just as fast toward me; One day, we will collide.

51.

What if you were to find out that everything you knew was wrong or misguided in understanding? Everything you've been taught; all that you believe? How would you cope?

Palpitations

52.

Observe your place. Understand your role in that moment. And, only speak when spoken to. Everything else is ego intervening.

53.

I imagine that the Vatican library is similar to the Library of Alexandria in that it contains the greatest collection of philosophical, theological and Divine thought as has been witnessed by man on Earth. Now imagine if that wellspring was accessible to everyone. Now, know what is was and what was is.

54.

Man strives for interstellar travel but fails to see that he can travel anywhere imaginable if he seeks to discover what is within.

Part 3 | Inspirations

55.

How would you grade yourself today versus yesterday? That is the only measurement that matters.

56.

Don't seek, but listen. Don't ask, but see. When you can acknowledge, follow. Any other action is just a wasteland for the ego.

57.

Medieval language was so simple yet mesmerizing in elegance and romance: "My lion. My lady. Your grace. I am yours and you are mine." Simplicity is elegance expounded.

Palpitations

58.

A soul mate is someone in whom a person recognizes harmony and resonance deep within the soul. There can be more than one – each spectacular in song.

59.

One must first find peace in solitude before spiritual harmony and earthly success can ever be obtained.

60.

A simple thing to do to make a difference: pay in cash to the self-employed, service-oriented person. Such a subtle effort removes the taxes and fees that most assume are accounted for within the cost of a service. This effort is like a drop of water in the ocean, for what is the ocean but the sum of all of the droplets of water.

Part 3 | Inspirations

61.

There's a certain duality to life. As bodies age and deteriorate, the spiritual journey leads us back home – to the origin of birth.

62.

Mankind has been blessed with the greatest of potentialities, but finds an oblivious peace somewhere in the awkward delivery and utilization of the wisdom which he has been imparted.

63.

Strive to be a "giver." But you can also be a "receiver" without being a "taker" – and that makes all the difference in the world.

Palpitations

64.

We only are blessed to keep what we are willing to let go.

65.

The purpose of the fall is to see where you were and where you were going from a different perspective. There's a reason for everything.

66.

The truest conversations occur with no masks, no veils, no embellishments; just the core on autopilot.

Part 3 | Inspirations

67.

I'm sure God has a sense of humor because humans must seem like really naive and innocent children in His eyes. I'm sure God has scratched his head at me from time to time and probably had a good laugh in the process. But, at least I made Him smile.

68.

Hearing does not require ears just as sight does not require eyes. We are not always spoken to through words.

69.

To feel the climb of the hill at the beginning of a great roller coaster ride is to know the anticipation of the spiritual journey. The ride is only fast and crazy in the awareness thereafter – but will take every breath away.

Palpitations

70.

The ability to see many meanings in something instantly is how man was intended to process the world around us.

71.

Dare to do something different every day. Change a life; change a moment for the better. Affect with change and therein affect the future.

72.

Few things in and of themselves are bad. It is the consequence of everything that unintentionally hitches a ride on the journey that wreaks havoc along the way.

Part 3 | Inspirations

73.

Clarity doesn't come with a roadmap.

74.

There's something about a piano driven song that draws me in and captures me for the duration of the conversation it wants to have with my soul.

75.

Ignorance is best defined as the point in time a person feels content with what they know and stops in their quest for further knowledge.

Palpitations

76.

To not feel judgment is the greatest release from the shackles of the world in which we live. Only in acceptance of this can a person begin to grow.

77.

Words are the vehicle for intention. Always hold close your words and stay true to what your words set in motion.

78.

If you can't control your emotions, you are probably addicted to them. That addiction is the same as for any other vice.

Part 3 | Inspirations

79.

The twists and turns of life will always lead the mind to question decisions past. But all along, everyone is always right where they belong.

80.

Nothing remarkable is ever possible without the removal of ego and in placing acceptance of all possible outcomes in the hands of our Creator.

81.

Anger is an expression of the ego's misunderstanding of life's greater picture and intention for each of us. Just breathe in, trust and relax.

Palpitations

82.

Someday it will all be perfect – but until then, the little reminders of everything that awaits ahead will always be beautifully humbling.

83.

The best moments are stuck in the middle of fast and slow – fast heartbeats, slow breath; fast rhythm, slow melody – and manage to encompass everything, every experience in life.

84.

In the eyes of a child a person grows younger – not older. Bear witness to the words of a child, for in their words is a truer wisdom than can be obtained through age.

Part 3 | Inspirations

85.

Whenever you face hard times and have seemingly insurmountable challenges in life, remember our Father's discipline is the greatest demonstration of His eternal Love.

86.

Stuck in the middle of the pendulum swing holding our lives together, patiently waiting, learning how to experience the bend in the plumb line.

87.

The journey of life is really multiple journeys concurrently traversed where time is irrelevant and truth is the greatest recognition.

Palpitations

88.

To release and let go is truly the greatest embrace.

89.

Life is but a brief whirlwind – an upside down, inside out, topsy-turvy kind of roller coaster ride.

90.

When the actions that demonstrate internal happiness are different from the picture the mind has created, change the picture – not the actions that embrace happiness.

Part 3 | Inspirations

91.

When a person calls someone crazy or says they have lost their mind, it merely emphasizes the judgmental's own inability to understand the greater facets of life.

92.

If someone or something captures my undivided attention, something is seriously wrong or either completely right.

93.

Earth is an amazing planet, majestic in nature. Yet most people spend the majority of time indoors and remain materialistic. Focus has been lost.

Palpitations

94.

Quite possibly, the greatest achievements in life can be produced from just a teaspoon of personal agony.

95.

Humans, en masse, mostly rely on collective reasoning, championing ego and materialism while lacking true individuality. Strive to differentiate yourself.

96.

What if instead of wealth, consciousness was held as society's highest value?

Part 3 | Inspirations

97.

Everyday is just a breath along the journey. From this viewpoint, my perspective has broadened exponentially.

98.

Ever think about the durability of bones? They survive hundreds of thousands of years (if not forever). The greatest manmade composites barely last 1000 years. From this point of view, the divinity in creation should be recognized and meditated upon.

99.

Today, technology is greater than mankind has seen in thousands of years. Culturally and spiritually though, we are far behind our elders.

Palpitations

100.

The greatest moments ever experienced do not have words spoken.

101.

True beauty hides in the flaws of people and things. If everything were perfect, nothing would be interesting. In imperfection, beauty is identified.

102.

Subtlety is an art and a strategic tool. If you are not a master of this art, the use of subtlety can easily be misinterpreted.

Part 3 | Inspirations

103.

There is a polar difference between reason seeking faith and faith seeking reason – the latter of which is where the greatest minds thrive.

104.

Don't capsize today's possibilities by being hung up on yesterday's tribulations.

105.

"Miracle" is a term for an occurrence of something greater than the average mind can comprehend.

Palpitations

106.

Sometimes there are overpowering moments that reassure us that life is not a convergence of great odds. In all ways, we are always right where we are meant to be.

107.

Impatience is fear of not controlling one's own destiny. So, let go. Embrace the ride and hold to faith in the destination.

108.

Nothing else matters when a person is on a crash course with the fast and rare moment ahead. This should be known as the present.

Part 3 | Inspirations

109.

I like to believe that when someone has an "old soul" that the meaning is more literal than most are taught to believe.

110.

Life is not just a convergence of great odds and chance encounters. Everything has a purpose, a reason, a plan.

111.

One of the hardest things is realizing personal growth is subject to a person's own ability to filter everyday noise from the truly extraordinary.

Palpitations

112.

You can't stop negative repercussions from creation. You can only hope to slow it down. To affect change, the negative must be given hope.

113.

Life is really about the rare. Otherwise, no experience would be worth having. No relationship worth starting. We long for the rare.

114.

Man's creations should only be seen as an assistant in learning how to harness nature's potential from within, not an "alternative to."

Part 3 | Inspirations

115.

Technology is just man's attempt at recreating something naturally achievable in every individual.

116.

The heart, mind, and soul all coexist in ways greater than most will ever know.

117.

Perception gained from presentation is just one of the oft overlooked approaches to success.

Palpitations

118.

The greatest leaders can remove ego yet still demonstrate confidence and knowledge.

119.

To live in the wonder, awe, and innocence of our magnificent world as a child sees it – if only for a moment – strive to see it like that again.

120.

Adversity is not the end of a journey, but the beginning of a wonderful story yet to be told.

Part 3 | Inspirations

121.

Looking back at the first years of my 30s, all I can do is smile and thank God for giving me the opportunity to learn who I always was and have always been within the core of my innermost essence.

122.

There is a distinct difference in being thankful and being indulgent by bragging/showcasing your blessings to everyone. Both cannot coexist

.

123.

Most people are pretty fragile, though they'd never let on. Words and even looks should always be treated as bricks through a glass window.

Palpitations

124.

If not in this experience, then in the next I know there is a broken perfection for everyone – but broken only to recognize the presence of perfection.

125.

I would rather be caught in this beautiful, mental andante than in the dissonance of reality.

126.

An instrumental song will invariably invoke a fabricated moment of broken perfection in the mind that will one day be experienced by the soul.

Part 3 | Inspirations

127.

She'll walk away unknowing, unaware that everyone caught in the afterglow of her presence has experienced a glint, a glimmer of her amazing.

128.

If you ever find yourself unhappy about something, find a way to change the situation or divest yourself in order to move onto something greater.

129.

The true beauty of a woman is in her eyes. Her body may age, but her real beauty will never fade.

Palpitations

130.

Superficial power is obtained by manipulating and shrouding truth. The irony is this is how the deceiver is deceived.

131.

The human language consists of only words with a tangible definition. Life is built around experiences that words can never truly quantify.

132.

The measure of success in the eyes of man is inherently flawed. True success is something most will never see nor care to understand, for success is not something that can be achieved through Earthly means.

Part 3 | Inspirations

133.

It is sad to see how many people are blind to the realities that bind them to the status quo. Politics, opinions, and voices all fall silent to the ears of God.

134.

All Earthly success is coupled with consequence. If consequence is inevitable, make sure the reason was worth it to the eyes of our Creator.

135.

I believe there is something greater waiting for us, something far greater than the mind can comprehend. Our time here is just a preparation.

Palpitations

136.

She must be beyond the typical to trigger intrigue...then it can become something more than amazing.

137.

To grow is to see past a person's strengths and weaknesses while realizing who they are within their core, understanding their ego, and amusing their will.

138.

I heard you laugh. I heard happiness. I heard the better part of life resonate in that moment.

Part 3 | Inspirations

139.

The inaudible melodies of our beings falling into harmony with one another all cognitively understood and visually represented in the mind...that is a heavenly song.

140.

Melodies are a lost art in modern music; for it is within the phrasing of emotions that messages become more than a melding of words and notes alone.

141.

Who you are is where ego resides, but what you are is who you are to our Creator – and nothing is more important.

Palpitations

142.

Find faith by fire, in water find reason, and unto the Earth, the wind of the Spirit shall meet.

143.

These are the four tenets: Faith is to fire. Water is to reason. Wind is to the spirit. Earth is to the human experience.

144.

For unto all, there is and will be one hundred and forty-four.

Part 3 | Inspirations

145.

Stop. Pause. Notice the motion inside you in this present moment – the motion that pushes and tugs at your core. Perhaps it is leading you somewhere. Perhaps it is telling you to remain at rest. Perhaps it is a feeling drawing you to a certain person, place or thing. The place beyond this awareness is where ego resides. Be still and know that the motion is leading you where you are meant to be – and have faith to follow. That is being. And, being is what this trip around the sun is all about.

146.

All summer I dread the arrival of cooler weather. But – then it gets here and I realize that it brings with it its own atmosphere that I've somehow forgotten. And then I remember I like it – I like it a lot. And so it is as in the journey through life that we tend to take the more comfortable road to the destination. So here's to fall, almost freezing temperatures at night, and brisk, see-your-breath mornings.

Palpitations

147.

To dream is to imagine. To believe is to allow our greatest dreams to become the potential for reality. Heart is how we dare to believe and allow ourselves to be but a vessel in helping those dreams become manifest in another's eyes. Those three principles form the strength in the walk: a journey in helping others while acting in the true spirit of light.

148.

There are times when parents must allow their children to have, do or endure something in order for the child to learn and grow. And so it is as in life and in all of the answers to questions sought. No person is more privy to the Cinderella ending than the next – rather though, to the next step that harvests growth for each person's step along the journey.

Part 3 | Inspirations

149.

If you really want to gain perspective on the world and those closest to you, look at antics that receive acknowledgement versus the deeds that go unnoticed – however worthy of praise in the eye of the Creator they may be – and remember, praise is fuel for the ego.

150.

I can't help but smile when I see happiness shine through those rare moments where someone inadvertently radiates their own Love for another through just a few simple words, a motion, or a subtle action. Those moments make me feel as if I've read a novel in just a few seconds of observance – as unintentional as it might have been.

Palpitations

151.

Sometimes everything in the world becomes apparent in one sweeping moment; and within that moment, the recognition of the journey and destination as one.

152.

Some see their past through the blinders of what could've been. But the truth is that the present moment is always what ever should've been – if a person can just take the time to see.

153.

A fish, once hooked, is not able to free itself under its own will. Only he who holds the rod can cause the fish to break loose or allow the line to become exhausted.

Part 3 | Inspirations

154.

Hidden within the moments of people reminiscing and reflecting on the greatest tragedies of our time is a greater foundational theme of compassion and Love for others. That oft overlooked theme buried within those moments is more important than these words can express. Many may never realize how something so tragic could be lined with a subtle calling toward goodness that is helping lead us all home. So now I tell you that everything – no matter how great or how tragic – will always have a lining in purpose and intent; clear to be recognized by those who desire to see, masked for those afraid of what may be unveiled. Fear is the driver of man's emotions. Faith is knowing what was there all along.

155.

Directional thoughts to influence a person's future are a product of the ego. As humans, all a person has is the personal experience of the present moment. The future is a concept – a path to acknowledge as a potentiality of existence while the present moment is all that will ever be experienced.

Palpitations

156.

Greatness to most is defined by relative achievements compared to other's failures. But greatness should not be viewed as a relative measure because relativity is merely a way to measure success. Greatness is an absolute that we must strive toward – and somewhere along the way, discover goodness, which will put us in the graces of greatness.

157.

There is never a reason to dislike another. There is only the recognition and acceptance of a person's shortcomings and the impetus to help guide them forward, or the recognition of one's own shortcomings and desire to grow. Think only in terms of teach/learn and learn/teach. Anything else is just taking the really long road to the eventual destination.

Part 3 | Inspirations

158.

Be a teacher to others, not a dictator. Be a leader, not a commander. Be a guidepost, not an obstruction. For in these actions, humility is acknowledged and freewill remains uninfringed.

159.

There are those who say, "Those who know how will always work for those who know why." But now I say, "The dependency on 'the why' and 'the how' neither leads nor follows. Both are cyclical in nature. Both create the momentum to move forward. There should be no higher value placed on one or the other, but rather on the overall impetus to move forward."

Palpitations

160.

The current state of affairs around the world is haunting. Unfortunately, the situation has become more dire than even the best efforts can rectify. The result will become an inevitable shift of individual minds seeking understanding. The beauty is that within the understanding, there is only a single truth that can shine through affecting the perceptions of all that has ever been and all that will ever eventually become. The day that humanity chooses not to see the material world for what it appears to be will be the tipping point to complacency's inertia.

161.

The human experience is a paradox wherein eagerness to learn causes a loss of recognition that the awareness of everything seen and unseen is both the answer and the question.

Part 3 | Inspirations

162.

Fear is the unwillingness to accept the potential of the unknown. Only in awareness of fear's psychological existence can the overarching message of life's journey be understood.

163.

Our lives are grounded on the impossible yet founded on the improbable. What a person thinks they know keeps them from truly knowing.

164.

The answer is in front of you – always. You don't have to look – just be.

Palpitations

165.

Life: such a rare and beautiful moment of art. In a word – stunning.

166.

Man will continue to try to create an alternative to biology though all he will find is that biology is already the most advanced science that can exist within the ecosystem of the Earth. Machines may rival, but only on a micro scale – not a macro scale.

167.

We are all just visitors here in this place, in this moment. Take advantage of the opportunity and embrace the destination. Leave your signature behind in a grand way.

Part 3 | Inspirations

168.

There's a moment a plane begins to lift its nose up and separate its wheels from the runway. Use that as an analogy to how the human experience should feel at any given point in time.

169.

Never seek out a job, but instead welcome in an opportunity that will allow you to refine who you are, your greatest strengths and your greatest weaknesses. If the right opportunity doesn't exist, be patient and keep listening, for it will appear.

Palpitations

170.

We are all unique individuals with unique abilities. Life is a canvas and part of a beautiful, grand design. Let your work speak for itself and strive to leave a mark on life's canvas in a way that only you could.

171.

Give it everything you have all over again. This time don't let it be reason seeking faith, but faith seeking reason – and that will make all of the difference.

Part 3 | Inspirations

172.

A man grows up and becomes a boy. This boy eventually grows into a child. As the child ages into a toddler, he one day looks into a mirror and sees the reflection of a young man with so much potential that has been squandered away...or has it? For the toddler has found himself staring into the mirror to see that he is a young man with so much potential.

173.

Unto space there is an awareness of everything around it. Unto a person staring into space, there is the observance of what seems like nothing. To be one with the universe a person must be both the observer and the observed while seeing everything and nothing at once.

Palpitations

174.

The hardest thing about leading is letting others decide to follow. Leading is passive, but is often mistaken for something that is actionable.

175.

Life is truly spectacular if you allow yourself to hear it, to see it, and experience it for what it really is.

176.

It is such a beautiful world. Today will be unlike any other and like no other to come. Teja.

Part 3 | Inspirations

177.

It is illogical to think that the soul begins at birth. For something that is eternal, cannot have a finite beginning as we are able to observe in this experience. It only makes sense that a soul has experienced other lives before – perhaps not on Earth, or perhaps not as human – but whatever the case may be, it would be irresponsible to allow ego to assert that a mortal is the creator of something infinite in existence.

178.

She moves with a grace as though she never touches the ground, gliding effortlessly through the expanses of my mind – revealing the sweetest truth. It's as though She was always there, patiently waiting for me to notice, though I had never stopped to see Her, to listen, to understand the significance of Her within my existence; Her very essence lifting me through the Heavens to see the unobservable greatness behind the veil of the human eye.

Palpitations

179.

People may ask for help, but rarely take it. Others may offer to help, but rarely do. The idea of helping is ego; the idea of needing help is ego. The action of helping is spirit; the action of receiving help is spirit.

180.

If you have surrendered unto the spirit and have removed ego from the situation, the spirit is then susceptible to both good and evil intentions based on spiritual influences. It is no longer mind over matter, but rather matter over mind. A strong mind may keep a person on the right path when ego is involved, but will be lacking spirit. But, for a spirit to be strong when ego is not involved, there must not be potentiality for negative polarization to seep in – for the mind is no longer in control and the spirit is un-polarized during its first years of growth during rebirth.

Part 3 | Inspirations

181.

Almost everything on Earth that begins has an ending. That is why it is so important to make the beginnings and the journey so much greater than the inevitable end – so it will all have been worth the ride.

182.

Everyone is learning to walk. A baby is never judged on its performance so why judge another? Instead catch them when they stumble and fall.

183.

At times we stumble. Sometimes we fumble and fall. But with eyes wide open, see those with outstretched arms because in them you will see Him.

Palpitations

184.

Only one concept transcends time, space and finite endings of earthly beginnings. That one concept is Love. So when you find it, treat it well. Nurture it. Revel in its grand presence and make sure to never let it go. It will take you across the universe and back if you let it.

185.

There are two types of nerves – one of which is rooted in ego's insecurities. The other is when one's spirit recognizes a spiritual counterpoint in another – the latter of which lenses the light to gravity's calling.

186.

To be hugged by an angel is one of the greatest feelings a soul can ever have.

Part 3 | Inspirations

187.

I have to believe the eyes are doorways to the soul. No other feeling is more powerful than when being locked in the gaze of the eyes of the one you Love.

188.

Her eyes fell into mine. Just as suddenly, my soul collided into hers. And in that moment, I saw our souls burst into a great light that illuminated throughout the greatest reaches of the heavens.

189.

I went to bed inspired. I awoke as if I had accomplished wonders – thoughts racing through my mind.

Palpitations

190.

When you see the world through the eyes of another, their spirit falls into view. Cherish the view and don't let go – for in it, is spectacular.

191.

Every person is bound to their own set of circumstances in life. Try to see the world through their eyes before you see it through your own.

192.

Your gravity is holding me in an orbit spinning around and around you. It's quite the site from this point of view, because I'm fading into you.

Part 3 | Inspirations

193.

Time is a mental barrier. The concept will only serve as a distractor on the journey to understanding.

194.

Gravity is a funny thing. Some objects hurtle toward Earth only to bounce off of its atmosphere. Others may burn up and fizzle into ashes before impact. But the rare collide in a moment of sheer brilliance – igniting the very surroundings in a stunning radiance; illuminating everything in a blanket of light.

195.

The demons we create are just ways that the mind tries to defy God's timing. And the truth is, He is always on time.

Palpitations

196.

To accomplish the unthinkable; to attain the unreachable – these concepts are clear within our grasp. To understand that science is only defined by those who have sought to define it so far, and that it will continue to be defined by the creative and determined minds of our present and future – let's be part of that imagination and those new defining moments that will positively affect the health and well-being of our future mankind.

197.

Life is an inspiration. We are the canvas. Each interaction in our daily lives is yet a new pigment used to compose the paintings of our own unique compositions. Every individual is a work in progress. Every person has a unique, genetic fingerprint – constantly evolving, constantly adapting.

Part 3 | Inspirations

198.

I stare into the blankness of a stark white page while music dances with my soul; the cursor blinking, gently asking me to write my thoughts. But my thoughts are already on another journey – a journey across the universe and back. When will they return? Who could possibly assert themselves to say they know…I'll just stay the ride and enjoy the view.

199.

Sometimes I can't help but sit back and let a song take my soul for a ride. Other times, it can happen from the movement of words I write. There will always be a need for both – to be a creator and also find surrender.

Palpitations

200.

The day we experience perfection is the day we pass through the eye of God's needle and see everything He has yet to reveal.

201.

Everyday is a blank page – yours to pen the story. So, make it one that others will read, be left inspired, given hope, and left feeling triumphant in the face of defeat.

202.

The brain is a bottleneck to the mind – thoughts flowing ad infinitum through the great sea of All That Is. Often I find myself lost in the wonder of the seas with little chance of putting that wonder into words once my thoughts move from the soul back to the mind.

Part 3 | Inspirations

203.

Truth is in finding the faith to believe in something greater than all.

204.

If your life were a movie, would it would end in a kiss and give hope to others?

205.

Doubt is a product of fear. Fear is a result of lack of faith. But with faith, neither shall enter the mind.

Palpitations

206.

The soul knows in an instant when it finds song in another. The rest of the time following that moment is just ego fighting to rationalize what the soul already knows.

207.

To Love like fire, to speak with laughter, to be held in another's thoughts, hopes and dreams – these are the signs of gravity calling.

208.

The space between two notes is where all of the grace is held; a beauty in the sustain of what once was, leading to what will one day become.

Part 3 | Inspirations

209.

Love wildly, Love strongly, Love passionately – unbridled by boundaries and convention; held in an orbit of certainty and peace in God's plan.

210.

Slowly, all of the faces on Earth turn to yours – like no else's exists but yours.

211.

To know the same blanket of stars covers us both up each night, and God's hands tuck us each in as we nod off to dreamland – Love impossibly.

Palpitations

212.

Someday, hindsight will reveal the story she was wrapped up in all along. For her, it will be quite the sight from that point of view.

213.

God's timing is immaculate. It will always be.

214.

To be Loved unconditionally, ferociously – a counter-force to the tide that rushes through the veins for another – that's the destination.

Part 3 | Inspirations

215.

The meaning of the sun and the moon, the North Star, the constellations traveling through the night sky – all can be found within the soul.

216.

Shooting stars in the night sky are like the language of the soul – marvelous in awe and wonder, where words are not required to know beautiful.

217.

Everything is just a whisper and a kiss away from peeling away at the seams to reveal the story that He intended for each of us to see.

Palpitations

218.

Home is where the soul finds its counterpoint in another; it is not a specific location or place to be. We all long to be home.

219.

There is something intimately special and spiritual about Pachelbel's Canon. Listen to it. Be a student unto its grand nature. It evokes the soul, calling it home.

220.

You can never Love too much. Love fast. Love hard. Love strong. When your time here is up, leave having Loved more than you were Loved.

Requisition

And so it is, as so it was – these are the melodies and palpitations of my heart anchored deep within my soul; to read – to breathe them in and welcome not just the words, but the melodies created within the soul, into the awareness of being. Within the walls of the body is a kingdom accessible by all for anyone willing to peer within. The effort to catch a glimpse of the Great All can appear so simple to the mind, for it is the eye of man that makes such efforts seem trivial. But, to catch a glimpse beyond the wall takes a more concerted effort than what the definition of the words entail. For the walk through the human experience is only relative to the walk of the spirit in so far as through conceptual metaphors.

In Earthly activity, we generate tangible results. In stillness, we learn the ways of the spirit. Between stillness and its capacity to generate abundance in all aspects of life, we humbly bear witness to the Great Divine. We are all called to be servants to the intention of Divine action. Some will hear the call. Some will pass through life oblivious to the call. Some will try to hear the call so much they miss the subtleness of its grand chorus. But within these words, these melodies, these inspirations and palpitations resonating within the depths of

Palpitations

the soul, a recognition of our great eternal Creator, God Almighty, resides. For so it was, and so it shall be – blessings unto Thee.

Teja.

Hallelu, Hallelu-jah. Praise to Lord God Almighty.

www.ingramcontent.com/pod-product-compliance
Lightning Source LLC
Chambersburg PA
CBHW021151080526
44588CB00008B/294